The Ethereal Escape

A collection of poetry

Shambhavi

First published in 2021 by
BecomeShakespeare.com

One Point Six Technologies Pvt Ltd,
123, Building J2, Shram Seva Premises,
Wadala Truck Terminus,
Wadala (E), Mumbai - 400037
T:+91 8080226699

ISBN: 978-93-5438-713-5

DEDICATION

For my parents.

ACKNOWLEDGEMENTS

Mamma, thank you for introducing me to the world of literature at the tender age of three. Your bedtime stories cultivated my interest in first reading and then writing. Thank you for pushing me to read books of all genres and encouraging me to write. You have nurtured my creativity and widened my horizons of thinking in more ways than you can imagine.

Papa, firstly thank you for bringing me tonnes of story books and novels while returning from your office trips. I still cannot describe my excitement when I saw the entire Winnie The Pooh collection in your hands twelve years ago. Secondly, if it wasn't for you, these pages would still be resting in my diary. Thank you for making this book a possibility.

I'd like to thank my teachers at school, especially Ms.Correa and Ms. Fernandes for fostering my interest in English Literature and believing in my potential.

Vrishti, thank you for patiently reading all my pieces and providing me with feedback that did not exceed a maximum of seven words. You will always be the first person I show my poems to. Pluto, I'm sorry for all the times I couldn't play with you since I was busy scribbling in my diary, you are my favourite sibling.

My grandparents and my great grandmother, your stories and experiences have inspired me in innumerable ways for which I can never thank you enough.

Divina, thank you for listening to all my poems on call, there is no one else I'd rather write poetry with. Zoya, this book would not have a title if it wasn't for you. Thank you for being even more excited about this than even I was. Serena, thank you for bringing some of these poems to life. Tista, Khushi, Tanisha, Pratyush, Rochelle and all my friends, thank you for your love and support, it truly means the world to me.

PREFACE

'Anime'- the Latin word for 'mind'. A million thoughts and ideas that call this one entity their home. The human mind encompasses a whole world in itself, a world that you can call your own. It is a structure that has seen no end, it is ever growing, constantly evolving.

The mind- our escape from the cruel world waiting outside, an escape whose route knows no direction, no end. An ethereal escape creating a galaxy within another. Just as the universe, where we are all visitors, the mind too is a guesthouse where each thought is a tourist. This book is a glimpse into my mind, my own little universe.

CONTENTS

THE BIG MAN ABOVE

The vast oceans,
The towering mountains
The grandeur of the green plains,
The roaring seas,
The twinkling stars
In the night sky,
The blooming flowers
And the animals that call
This planet their home.
The blazing sun and the glistening moon-
He made them all
With tender care
And a hint of sparkle
That made each of them shine in their own unique way.
And then,
He created you.

The Big Man knew
That the world needed one of you too.
It in all its perfection,
It needed your flaws,
Your mistakes,

Your imperfections.
It needed your angelic presence,
Your smile,
The twinkle in your eye
And your kind, kind heart.

In His giant book,
He printed you as a chapter,
Not just to be flipped,
But to be read,
To be understood.
So begin your story,
The world awaits
As you write it
And He smiles from up above
On his favourite creation.

Illustrated by: Sphurti Patil

LIGHTNING

She loved the rain,
How every drop that braced the earth,
Relieved it from its pain.
It had been during the rains,
That they had first frivolously danced around,
Twirling, giggling and jumping into little puddles,
Of nothing but joy.

Every season that nature bestowed,
Became serene, if it was for his presence.
But the sun! Oh, the sun!
She once caught him gazing at it and asked,
"What captivates you to such an extent,
That you're staring right into its blazing fire?"
"It'll never forsake you,
Even when it sets,
You know it'll rise again.
It'll test you for a while,
Because it knows
That you'll survive through the night.
To assure you of its guidance,
It'll leave behind the light of the moon,

As you find your way
Through the darkness.
But it will never, never abandon you", he said.
And so she was convinced,
That their love was like the sun too,
Forever bright,
Forever brilliant,
Forever blazing,
Eternal.

Illustrated by: Shambhavi

But nature has its seasons,
And so did their love.
This time,
Instead of the rain,
They witnessed lightning.
And in that moment, that dreaded moment,
She forced herself to believe,
That their love wasn't the blissful rain or the delightful
sun,
It was lightning.
The lightning that occurs,
When it wishes to-
But when it does,
It lightens up the whole damn sky.
Even if it's for a millisecond,
In that moment,
Nothing shines brighter,
Neither the sun, nor the rain, nothing.
Only lightning.
That was their love,
So pure that every time it struck,
Even the majestic sky forgot its darkness.
But it brought along with it thunder-
The anxiousness of her beating heart,
Unaware of when lightning would strike next.
But that's all that thunder does right?
Waits for lightning to make a reappearance?
Waits for it to brighten the sky yet again?
So that is what she does now,
Like thunder,

Keeps the memories of the sun and the rain,
Protected in her heart,
And waits for her love to take birth again.
Even if it's for a short time.
For that is all that matters,
For that is all she wants,
That one bolt of lightning.

THE HOTEL

'Every morning- a new arrival,
A joy, a depression or
Simply a void.
Welcome them all.
A crowd of sorrows,
Or a throng of wide grins.
My doors cease to seal
As I am grateful
For each soul who chooses to enter
Through my almost towering gates.
For each has been been sent as a letter from above,
To learn from me,
To enlighten me,
To change me.

Illustrated by: Sphurti Patil

THE UNIVERSE

Fascinating, intriguing, enchanting.
In all its entirety,
Each of its atoms tell a story.
Each molecule represents a soul.
The millions of stars and suns its encompasses-
A million different entities,
A million different structures,
A million different worlds.
Yet, we all seek solace in the universe-
It's peace,
It's tranquility,
Is something so divine,
That we all desire it.
Isn't it beautiful,
That an ocean of bodies so vast, so complex
Has a special place for each and every one of us-
A letter from above,
For all of us.
Shouldn't that be enough?
That sense of belonging,
To know that we are cherished,
Treasured and loved.

For we belong to the universe,
It is what moulds us.
It is looking upon us.
Directing our every move,
Showering us with love and care,
And nurturing us all-
One by one;
In this life and beyond.

Illustrated by: Sphurti Patil

SHE

(The Mahabharata is an ancient Indian epic conceived by Sage Vyasa. While it boasts of imparting values of duty, morality and salvation, it has more often than not subjugated its female characters to a position of inferiority. Be it Draupadi, the daughter of the holy fire or Amba, the Princess of Kashi. Here, I write of yet another woman, 'Uttara', who had been repressed by the clutches of patriarchy throughout her life.)

Born in the lap of towering dunes,
Where the glittering sand outshines the sun.
She is the sweet rain,
That brings life to the desert.
She is the Princess of Viratanagar[1].

She cushions herself upon her father's knee.
Her mother notices that her tresses haven't been combed.
She calls out to her, but our heroine escapes,
Her hair, messy, tangled, unabashed.
She is the daughter of King Virata[2] and Queen Sudeshna.[3]

---

[1] Modern day Bairat, a town in northern Jaipur, Rajasthan, India
[2] King Virata was the king of the Matsya Kingdom, in whose court the Pandavas spent a year in concealment during their exile.
[3] Queen Sudeshna was the wife of King Virata.

The ground beneath feels the spring in her stride,
The sand carves a path for its Princess,
While the air carries her spirit, in every sand particle
That finds its way into the threads of her carefully woven
cerulean skirt.
Escaping from the world's vanity,
She lands in her lair,
Where her toys are hidden-
Hidden, might you ask?
Well, stitched dolls with crystal blue eyes
Never could cast their spell on her.
For she only ever looked upon her wooden soldiers,
With little fishes[4] engraved on their vermilion headgears.
She wished to swing swords, fight battles and wrestle with
wild boars.
She'd run to her brother every time he'd return from war,
And instead of nursing each scar, she'd ask the story behind
every wound.
After all, she was the sister of a warrior.
She was the sister of Prince Uttar.

---

[4] A 'matsya' or a fish was the symbol of the Matsya Kingdom.

Illustrated by: Serena Augustine

When she wasn't busy debating with *Gurus* in court,
Over matters in which' girls shouldn't meddle with anyway,'
She'd exhibit her emotions through dance.
The form of expression that empowered her,
Her inhibitions concealed,
Her voice heard (or maybe not)
But she assumed that in an audience of a hundred,
At least one would discern the fire in her eyes.
The people exclaimed that their Princess was born to dance,
As her body swayed like the waves against the seashore.
A courtier declared,
"Her movements will put the *apsaras* [5]to shame,
Not that I'm surprised,
She is *Brihannala's* [6]disciple".

Dark clouds hover over the golden desert,
Trumpets sound ,the fragrance of *mogras* and roses fill the
air,
The city dances with fervour,
As their princess is getting married!
"To Arjuna!", a handmaid exclaims.
Chaos waves away the jubilance
As questions are asked,
While answers seem to be none.
"How can that be ?*Arjuna* is *Brihannala* [7]in disguise!

---

[5] Celestial dancers
[6] Arjuna ,a Pandava was disguised as Brihannala during his stay in Viratnagar
during the final year of the Pandavas 'exile ,where he was a dance and music
teacher for Uttara.
[7] A Pandav Prince ,the third son of Pandu and Kunti

The Gods forbid marriage between a *Guru*[8] and a *shishya*".[9]

The depths of the lines on the King's forehead can be measured,
His frown now runs deeper between his brows,
The alliance has been announced
And *Arjuna* has refused -for how can he wed his own student.
Tensions rise ,a Princess's reputation is on the bet.
Virata prays ,he kneels ,he begs,
When finally *Arjuna* offers his son's hand in marriage to the Princess.
"*Abhimanyu* [10]!Oh the glorious ,the brave Prince *Abhimanyu*,
Our family couldn't be happier"!
Truth be told,
In that moment,
The King would've married his daughter
To any of *Pandu*'s[11] kin,
To preserve his daughter's honour,
The fact that it was *Abhimanyu*,
Was just a boon.

As rumours fly
And relations are established,
Our princess doesn't let a tear stream.

---

[8] Teacher
[9] Student
[10] Arjun and Subhadra's son and Lord Krishna's nephew
[11] Pandu was the King of Hastinapur and the father of the Pandavas.

But her brain won't stop pounding,
Brihannala ,a woman till the day before,
Was indeed *Arjuna* ,a Prince in hiding.
His disciple till the day before,
She would now wash his feet,
As his daughter-in-law.
From *Arjuna* to *Abhimanyu,*
From father to son,
Like a commodity,
From one buyer to another.
Just as how she traded her toys,
She was now one of them.
A toy.

Her hair braided-
Her wild locks have now been tamed.
From a light mint ,a deep ,passionate crimson adorns her.
She transforms from a chirpy maiden to a mature woman
Almost overnight.
A little girl who chased kites,
Is now a bride.
She is the wife of *Abhimanyu.*

A month into their marriage,
Instead of laying out silken robes
On a flower strewn bed,
She presents a shield and a mace to her husband.
The devastating war of Mahabharat rages.
She wishes for him to stay
And caresses his bushy hair as she stares into his tender

eyes.
For the millionth time she pleads to let her accompany him,
He cups her face in his scarred hands and says,
"The battlefield isn't for you my dearest,
Wear your brightest colours and await
As your husband returns victorious".
And yet again,
She feels like a doll,
When she wished to be a warrior.

The thirteenth day of war,
The sky is a flaming orange.
She bids her warrior off to war
As she ties an armlet of five precious stones,
To protect him from his own kith and kin.
She looks at him one last time,
A strange feeling grips her.
His horse gallops away,
Leaving only dust behind,
And a void within her heart.

It feels like a long day,
Almost unending.
Although the hollowness of her heart hasn't recovered,
She feels something blossom,
As if she's nurturing a bud within her-
Creating a life.
And it is confirmed
When the nursemaid declares
That the shoes of a father

Now belong to Abhimanyu.
Barely fifteen,
Her mind encompasses millions of feelings,
And she finally chooses delight,
As she will give birth to one of the *Pandu* clan's heirs.
The war camp metamorphosizes into a hall of celebration,
But it seems incomplete,
Her eyes search for her husband.
Little does she know,
That the little foetus
Is the last she has left of him.
The thirteenth day of war,
She is a pregnant widow.

Wails and cries echo in the camp,
The *Pandavas* 'dearest son
Has begun his journey to the beyond.
As piles of the dead are burnt,
And dark grey whiffs of smoke build castles in the air,
She weeps,
With no one else to blame but fate.
As she sees her husband's body surrender to the pyre,
She feels a hand on her shoulder ,hoping for some solace.
But hope was something she should've long forsaken
For the Queen mother says,
"Cry my dearest ,but in your chamber,
If you cry amidst the other widows
They'll lose courage too.
Choose bravery ,my child".
She can neither shed a tear,

Nor drown herself in grief,
As people look up to her,
She is the daughter-in-law of the *Pandavas*.

The war finally sees an end,
Kurukshetra[12] is now painted red,
Bodies of warriors who once boasted of their strength,
Lie with abandoned spirits.
Victory belongs to the *Pandavas* ,they say.
Their faces not reflecting that very fact.
Their sons deceitfully killed
By the cruel *Brahmin* whose forehead wears a silver stone.
She rests in her room,
Stroking the cavity that envelops her unborn child.
Her only reason to live.

The night falls
Rain pounds on the thatched roofs
The wind howls ,wolves cry
And the sky trembles in fear
As lightning strikes.
She wakes up ,shivering
Pearls of sweat sit on her forehead
As the same inkling fills her heart,
When she saw *Abhimanyu* ride away.
Chaos races on in her mind-
She'd lost everything that was dear to her-

---

[12] The war of Mahabharata is believed to have taken place here ;modern day city in Haryana

Her land ,her childhood ,her brother ,her husband ,her joy.
The only one she had left
Hadn't even seen the face of this world.
Lost in distress,
She is woken
By *Ashwathama* ,[13]as he roars into the universe,
To kill the last of *Pandu*'s clan
And she shrieks ,she yells ,she screams-
Her unborn child.

The ones who survived the war land in her room,
Subhadra [14][15]and *Draupadi* [16][17]calm her down.
Forests flame,
Animals bellow,
The sun and the moon disappear
And the sky tears apart,
As the *Bhramastra* [18]pierces her womb.
She knows it is the end.
And then,
There is silence.

---

[13] The son of Dronacharya ;the one who killed the Pandavas 'sons deceitfully to avenge the death of his friend Duryodhana.

[14] Lord Krishna's sister and Arjuna's second wife

[15] Arjuna's wife and Lord Krishna's sister

[16] The one who emerged from the Holy fire ,Drupad's daughter and the Queen wife of the Pandavas.

[17] The one who rose from the holy fire ,King Drupad's daughter and the wife of the five Pandavas.

[18] A weapon created by Lord Brahma and is considered to be one of the most destructive weapons mentioned in Hinduism.

Illustrated by: Serena Augustine

Her eyes shut,
But she hears *Kunti*[19] speak.
She's told to wake up
For she carries the heir of the *Pandavas*,
The last of their lineage.

But not once ,not once
Does anyone in the room
Ask for her.
If her unborn child was secure,
She knew her now disfigured ,blood washed body
Would be left to the mercy of vultures.
And for the first time,
Anger rages within her,
Who was she?
The Princess of *Viratanagar* wouldn't have mastered the *Vedas*,[20]
King *Virat*'s daughter wouldn't dare leave her hair untied,
Prince *Uttar*'s sister would never touch her brother's wooden armies,
Abhimanyu's wife would never need a sword in her husband's presence,
The *Pandavas* 'daughter-in-law wouldn't express an emotion
So ,who was she?

Images flash in her mind-
Sweet music ,graceful gestures and flowing hair,
Holy books and the *Vedas*,
Silver swords and a free mind,

---

[19] The mother of the Pandavas
[20] A large body of religious scriptures.

Wild kites and wooden soldiers,
And a kind ,beautiful heart.
She was Uttara.
A daughter ,a wife ,a Princess,
But first a woman.
First ,*Uttara*.

She finally awakens from her deep slumber.
It feels like an eternity has passed.
Her lifeless son lies beside her.
She weeps bitterly
And questions *Krishna*[21] the purpose of her life.
Her answer is heard as He directs the *Sudarshan*[22]
At the perished child
And a cry is heard.
The cry of a newborn baby.
"Your purpose was to carry this child,
You ,my dear ,are the reason that the *Pandu* legacy will live on,
Your son will righteously rule *Hastinapur* [23]in the years to come.
Parikshit -the one who has stood the test of death.
You are the mother of *Parikshit-*[24]"

"STOP!
Oh Lord!

---

[21] Worshipped as the eighth incarnation of the Hindu god Vishnu and is also known as the supreme God.
[22] The Sudarshana Chakra is a spinning ,disk-like weapon having 108 serrated edges used by the Hindu god Vishnu or Krishna.
[23] Capital city of the Kuru Kingdom ;modern city in Uttar Pradesh
[24] The son of Uttara and Abhimanyu and Yudhistir's heir to the Kuru throne

If you utter these words,
Then what hope do I have from these mortals?
Lord you are witness-
All my life ,I have been treated as everything but human
When I faced Arjuna's rejection,
When I was passed down to Abhimanyu,
When I was only married
To give *Yudhistir* [25]his heir,
When I was only protected
So that this child could live.
Oh Lord ,*Parikshit* is the son of Uttara,
Parikshit ,whose mother was born only to give him birth,
Whose mother didn't see a childhood for him,
Whose mother got married into a clan ,just to give them
their Prince.
The *Brahmastra* that destroys the universe,
She endured its wrath for him.
Parikshit's life is built upon *Uttara's* sacrifice ,*Uttara's* pain.
And *Uttara's* life?
I dare call it a life-
Virata's daughter ,*Uttar's* sister
Arjun's daughter-in-law ,*Abhimanyu's* wife,
Parikshit's mother,
But never ,never *Uttara*.
For this Lord ,I will never forgive you.

Who am I?
Answer me Lord!
Your silence is not the answer I seek"!

---

[25] Eldest brother of the Pandavas

And for the first time,
Krishna is speechless.

PHOTOGRAPH

I lie on a wall,
Wearing an ornate golden frame,
Among several others
Decorated the same way.
I'd like to think though,
That I am special.
And as you stop by the corridor
To tell my story
To each guest who passes by,
I smile.

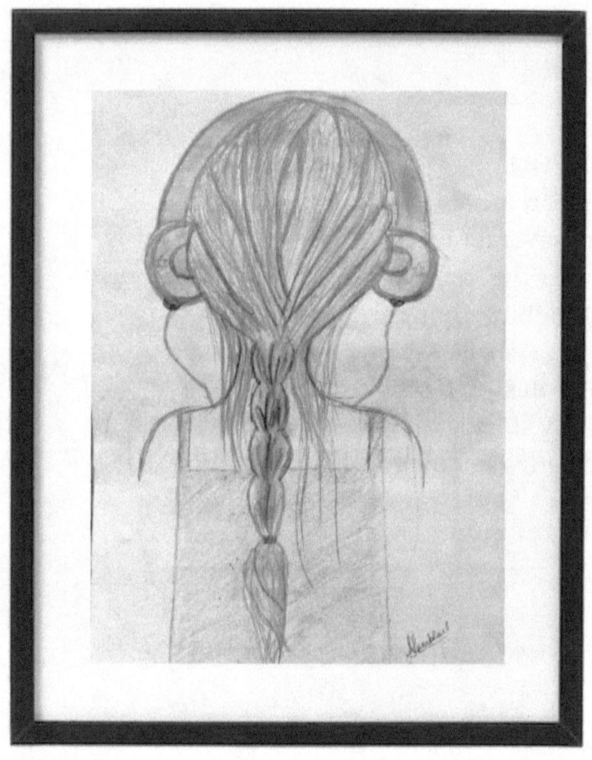

Illustrated by: Shambhavi

SMILE

It's insane how much a smile can weigh.
It possesses the power to transport you,
To a world where only joy and abundance
Build their homes.
It can make you fall in love,
Such is the power
Of a smile.

It may not necessarily be from a loved one-
When an old lady
Cherishing the simplest of moments with her grandson
Flashes her aged broken-whites at you,
She's sharing a slice of her soul with you.
When the liftman nods and smiles
As you enter the lift-
His home for the day,
He forgets that he hasn't paid his daughter's school fees
yet.
When a soldier's mother is on the phone with her son,
And her lips twist into a wide smile
Which reaches the end of her cheeks,
The pride and relief she feels,

Makes your eyes swell too.
When a father who's bidding farewell to his beloved
daughter at her wedding
Blinks away his tears
And a sad smile peeks through his grey moustache,
His grief pierces your heart,
While he forgets for a second,
That his daughter's heart will be someone else's now.

A smile tells a story,
From one heart to another.
It conveys feelings,
That words never could.

Illustrated by: Serena Augustine

One muscular movement,
But in that moment,
All your worries, burdens and anxiety-
Seem alien.
A smile engulfing warmth,
May seem trivial
But it is the divine path
That leads to a glimpse
Into one's soul.

A mere five letter word
But such massive is its force
That it binds together,
You and me,
The young and the old,
The rich and the needy,
The loved and the heartless.
In this colossal, yet cruel world,
It brings us all a little closer.
Sharing little fragments of ourselves
It connects us in a way,
That nothing, absolutely nothing can.
So, smile,
For it is
Nothing but magic.

THE MOON

Selenophilia-
Love for the moon.
The moon that shuns it pride
And borrows light
From the orange, blazing ball of fire
To shine for us mortals.
The moon that plays with mere clouds
To let the sky frolic.
The moon that smiles upon us
When roads are dark
And forests are quiet.
The moon whose eyes are alien to rest
As it stays awake
While the world sleeps.
The moon, my friend
Who's calm soothes my soul
The moon, who I ask
For a promise-
A promise to nurture you,
A promise to bless you,
A promise to bind you and me.
In this life or the next.

And I smile
As the moon shines.

Illustrated by: Serena Augustine

MEMORIES

I rest in your heart
And I have
For years together
Without a sole intrusion.
I smirk
Because manipulation is my game-
One, your mind and I have played
Innumerable times.

Remember the boy
Who shattered you
To an object of disdain
Then apologized with pink roses,
And you smiled and forgave him?
That was me.
When you wanted to bloom afresh
And leave the sandy soil behind
But couldn't...?
You tried several escapes
But darling,
I breathe in you
If only you could flee from me.

As long as I live
Your past will always play its part.
Try and obliterate my existence
But my footprints will never erase,
They will only engrave themselves deeper.

I am, however
Not the antagonist you think of me-
The images you swipe
In front of your eyes
Of beloved friends and family
When they seem far,
That is me.
When you're exhausted of being old,
You think of the times
You converted a tent into a palace
With torches as soldiers,
And you laugh.
That is me.
When sorrow engulfs your soul
And you look at
The photographs on your wall
Of places you've been
And folks you've met,
You smile.
That is me.
So you see,
I make you laugh,
And I make you cry.
Such is my might.

Dear one,
I am your past,
Building a home in me
Would be a fool's mimicry.
For I am only a getaway,
Your getaway
From the present.

Illustrated by: Sphurti Patil

THE STARS ARE PROUD

Isn't it strange
That these trivial balls of fire
High above in the night sky
A million miles away,
Know all our secrets?
All our fears,
Insecurities, dreams and aspirations.
They've been here since the very beginning,
And they've witnessed it all.
They've moulded you,
As you grew, fell and rose again.

The stars know you're invincible.
They've seen a fire blaze within you,
Just as their own.
They've been there,
As you conquered wars with yourself,
And this cruel, cruel world.
They believe in your wrath, in your power.
They have faith in you.
They'll silently cheer when you are at your peak
And console you when you've hit rock-bottom.

You are an embodiment of the phoenix,
They know you will rise from the ashes
And shine brighter than ever.
For they are a testimony of your journey,
They've seen you grapple,
Seen you struggle,
Seen you succumb,
Seen you scrape through, even.
Seen you fight,
And seen you evolve.
They have seen you,
Acknowledged you
And they are proud of you.
The stars are proud of you.

Illustrated by: Serena Augustine

CANVAS

Life is a spectrum of colours.
Let those shades be of the present.
Pigments of orange and red,
Of sanctity and love
Of yellow and green
Of freshness and prosperity
Of blue and purple
Of growth and evolution
And of black and white,
Of turmoil and calm.
But in the canvas of life,
Can the hues of the past
Be forgotten?

Illustrated by: Sphurti Patil

THE FAVOURITE

To you,
I am nothing more than a string of bells.
Trinkets secured on cotton cord.
Insignificant. Trivial.
For her,
I am her favourite ornament.
I speak not from arrogance
But mere facts.

I've seen it-
Seen it in her eyes
When she runs around
And the walls of her house echo
With my sweet sound.

Seen it when her hands
Wearing circles of a bright carmine colour
Hold me with almost a motherly affection.

Seen it when she refuses to look at any other of my kind
Because I was her first love.
When she ceases to toss me away

Even if I was the one who caused
The red scars on her feet.

Seen it when I'm tied
Above her ankles
When she sways her feet
With utmost grace
So that I sound my best.
Strange isn't it?
Caged around her feet,
Is when I feel most free.

You see
Maybe I'm more than an accessory.
I am a part of her
An organ she chose.
I am her ghungroo
I create the rings
She wishes me to
But she is the only master I'd choose
Again.
And again.
For eternity.

Image credits: Khushi Hanspal

RED

Bangles and bracelets of gold
Clad her hands.
She stands at the threshold of a new life
Adorned in a deep crimson.
As she dips her feet
In a potion of red
The colour of love,
Little does she realise
That her feet will engrave
Marks of the same red
When they're left behind
In a pool of blood.

LIFE AND DEATH

She lies on the hospital bed,
The doctor shakes his head.
Surrendering.
He turns to the two
Who gifted life to her.
They know it is the end.
They sit in the aisle.
Along with those,
Who loved her and wished her well.
They've let go,
Letting her soul transition
Into the beyond.

He walks in.
All eyes turn to him.
He's let into the ICU.
Unable to gather the strength
To set his eyes upon her.
The colour drained from her face,
Her vibrance vanished.
The lips, that only ever twisted into a smile,
Are now clasped.

The ears, that perked up every time she heard his name,
Are now still.
The strands of hair that always framed her face,
Are now neatly tucked.
The hands, that were only ever raised to help,
Are now motionless.
The eyes that only knew love,
Are now sealed.

He goes over to her,
Stares in disbelief,
Unable to fathom,
That the glistening moon of his dark, night sky
Is now a pale, icy blue corpse.

He sheds a tear,
Closes his eyes
And places his hand
Onto something of hers
He will have for eternity.
A part of her,
That will never leave his side.
Her heart.

A machine beeps.
A heartbeat is heard
And her eyes flutter.

Illustrated by: Sphurti Patil

THE CLASSROOM

The morning sun shines yet again,
Relentlessly.
The bell cries
As the tong is struck.
The classroom contains its
Doors wide open,
Welcoming us all.
To learn,
To seek,
To conquer.

But what would this classroom be
Without the bricks who build it?
Each student, a symbol, an experience.
The loud, talkative one,
With the wind flying in her hair.
One glimpse at her-
A reminder that your life is nothing less than a carnival of
joy.
The one who has scribbled notes for the world to see-
That will to give
You will realise,

Is the drive you need to truly live.
The shy boy peacefully seated in a corner,
Your urge to reflect-
That your heart isn't meant to be displayed,
But its feelings, to be felt.
The one who'd drown in an ocean of books
For mankind, in all it's years
Hasn't found a substitute for hardwork.
The one who's staring out of the window,
Looking at a mere cloud float across the sky,
For dreaming is indeed,
The sailor of your voyage.

The teacher,
For learning is a journey
That has seen no end.
The helper-
The one you should offer
A neatly wrapped gift of gratitude,
For she is an angel with a broom.

The one who commands the attention of the entire room,
Who will not have a single face turn away,
Tolerance is what you need, my friend.
In that moment, and in many more.
Your life will not always present,
The rides you choose.
Finally, the one who's eyes you meet
And your heart forgets its primary function,
To insist,

That to live, is to love.

Is the classroom any different from life,
I ask?
Each event,
The beginning of a new lesson
Each character,
A guide from beyond
Each experience,
A form of realisation.
Every crack of dawn,
A new advent
To seek life,
To seize it,
To laugh at it,
To love it.

Illustrated by: Sphurti Patil

BLISS

She sits by the windowsill,
The world beyond
Spins a web of chaos
Her eyes glisten
And shine with reassurance
And convince me
That she won't fall prey to it.
A frown appears
On someone insignificant-
"Is she lonely?"
A cuckoo cries outside
As if to say,
"No, she is in bliss,
The bliss of solitude."

Illustrated by: Sphurti Patil

BEHIND CLOSED DOORS

The lights click
And everything is dark.
The sun has set,
And nests are full.
Behind closed doors
Are written millions of stories,
A myriad of which,
I will tell today.

The curtain is drawn
And a pair of eyes peek from behind.
A little bright eyed girl
Chooses her midnight snack.
Innocence and mischief engulf her
As the night falls.

A floor above,
Lights of yellow and blue blink
As a boy drowns himself
In a world of firing guns and blazing buildings.
His escape from this world
That has already done him too much harm.

A scream of joy is heard
As somewhere on the eighth floor
A toddler takes his first steps,
His mother cries
While the father declares this news
To enlighten the sleeping world
Of his little one's first medal.
Whilst their tears are of joy,
Their neighbours weep all night
Weep because, a grandmother saw heaven
Before she witnessed the birth of her own granddaughter.

Illustrated by: Sphurti Patil

While two celebrate togetherness
Staring at the stars,
Another sleep with their eyes open,
Turning away from each other
Blaming no one
But only the universe for their fate.

And then,
There is me.
Me who sits by my window,
Me who stares into the worlds of the unknown
To escape from my own.
Me who has learnt
That those feelings aren't even our own,
Manipulated by a force
Far greater than us
For the universe writes the stories
Behind closed doors.

THE UNIVERSE'S BETRAYAL

They refuse to cross
Each other's paths
The universe though, is cruel.
It brings them together
On the lines that run parallel forever
But little does it realise
That parallel lines never meet.

Illustrated by: Shambhavi

STRANGERS WITH MEMORIES

The tempestuous rain pounds on the roof,
And the wind howls,
It's cold.
The snow glitters
From the light of the windows above,
The branches of trees are bare,
The barks seem to shiver too
And the moon wears a blanket of clouds.
As crisp, dry leaves fall to death,
A bud takes birth again.

She enters the coffee shop,
The door closing behind her.
A few strands of her hair float,
While the rest are neatly tied,
Damp from the cold outside.
The little bells of her bracelets jingle,
As she chooses a table in the corner.
The fog that had settled on her jet-black glasses
Soon disappears,
As if preparing her
For the future she is going to envision.

His boots cast mucky footprints behind
As he admits himself into the shop,
Leaving the waitress annoyed.
His olive green coat swinging by his side.
He ruffles through his hair,
Giving his waves
A chance to breathe.
He reclines on his chair,
Flexes his muscular arms, stands up with a jerk
And walks towards the cold, marble counter.

As the aroma of steaming cappuccinos fills the cafe,
She senses something different.
The air seems familiar,
A scent that she can call home.
Cocoa beans certainly don't have that effect on her,
Neither do damp coats hanging near the door.
The coffee machine churning at the back
Doesn't seem to fade her thoughts away.
She can feel it.
A second later, she knows why.

She hears a deep laugh,
A sound that her heart remembers all too well.
She turns behind.
His face covered,
But her eyes don't miss the craters on the sides of his
cheeks
The dimples she'll never forget.
No, it's the cold,

Its an illusion
The games her heart frequently plays with her.
But almost like an involuntary reaction,
Like a force guiding her from above,
She reaches for the pillar, behind the counter.

A voice rings in his ears.
It isn't his.
But it is of someone he called his own.
He feels dizzy,
Not the sick-dizzy
The kind of dizzy,
He can't describe.
He needs to pay for his order,
His hands shiver as his hands find their way into his back
pocket,
It's not from the cold though
It's from the feeling that is new..but not alien.
And then, he notices from the mirror kept on the counter,
Floating strands of hair
Forming patterns his eyes have already seen.
He can predict her movements,
He knows she'll alter her stance in a moment.
And she does.

Illustrated by: Sphurti Patil

He can't see her face,
But he knows her.

She moves further,
Her blush pink cardigan brushes against his coat.
She pulls her arms close together
To hide the goosebumps
Who's cause for appearance, she doesn't know.

She looks ahead,
For a better look at the menu.

He looks behind,
For he can't find his wallet.

And then.

Their eyes meet,
Their souls awaken
And they are no longer strangers.
They are the few,
Who are strangers with memories.

Shambhavi is a seventeen year old currently studying in the twelfth standard at Bombay Scottish School, Mahim and will further be pursuing English Literature and Media Studies.

This book is a collection of the poetry and musings she has penned down over the past couple of years.

She enjoys painting, baking, dancing, and is a trained Bharatanatyam dancer. She aspires to become a filmmaker in the future and stays in Mumbai with her parents, sister and her dog, Pluto.

Write to Shambhavi:

Email: sshambhavi056@gmail.com

Instagram: shambhavi_1106

www.ingramcontent.com/pod-product-compliance
Lightning Source LLC
La Vergne TN
LVHW091618170726
843492LV00007B/2494